BIRTHRIGHT

BIRTHRIGHT

KENDEL HIPPOLYTE

PEEPAL TREE

First published in Great Britain in 1997
Peepal Tree Press Ltd
17 King's Avenue
Leeds LS6 1QS
England

ISBN 094883 95 5

CONTENTS

'I WILL LIFT UP MINE EYES...'

The rich man, near the summit, looks
through the needle's eye

down on the nouveau riche
blustering up hill, all brass and flash

glancing, in the rear-view mirror,
at the middling aspirer behind

who, despite his straight or crooked efforts
won't ever reach the summit

but at least is pleased (thank God)
that he is not so far below

as the worker, struggling from a rut
into a blindman's ditch, and cursing at

all unemployed and thieves and beggars
the normal litter spawned in any sty

who yet believe that even they
fit in somewhere, therefore are better than

the shocking madman on the dung-heap
who laughs and understands the whole thing

SYSTEMATOMIC HEGEMONEY

it is a system
it is macro- and micro-economic, macro-demonic on the skyline,
        spreading beyond eye and sense
it is intestinal; minute viruses grinning in the convoluted
        canals of the psyche
it is old men, slumped like bags in corners, abused beyond use,
        not even worth insulting
it is children who rose like kites in February, and in April
        hung from electric wires like the broken bodies of birds
it is the faded tattering of these skeletonic things of beauty,
        only the ribs left
it is the song of childhood persecuted to a scream
it is the city's buildings, catatonic, refusing back the sun's light,
petrifacting into maniacal monoliths, the elevators
        suck-and-sighing obscenely up and down inside them
it is history with a diminutive 'h' trying to pump belief
        into itself

II

but the dollars are whispering;
last week John Day committed suicide, slitting his wrist with
        a five-dollar bill
Joseph screwed Marianne again, using a rolled up twenty for a condom
the pound this month went down, the union jack went with it;
the dollar is up on the flag pole conducting the national anthem
some white ghost shuffling at the corner of the eye in
        bedroom slippers, computing the fiscal digitalia,
        is crafting a necklace of bones around you
        but the dollars are whispering — per capita!
        'nother head lopped off   — per capita!

whatsa time, whatsa time? — per capita!
'nother fuck? Coming up — per capita!
stuff that baby back inside, seal up the wombs,
per capita won't allow it, can't afford it;
fiscal policy and budgetary control are taking a stroll, inspecting
the tenement yards for unapproved love-stains, for illegal tender
they are installing slot-machines between the legs of love-lost
women, whore mothers and rub-a-dub players
whose tears are secrets, like pearls
Gross National Product is rolling down the road, flattening
the workers into barbergreen and sand, creating a
smooth surface for the flow of multinational traffic;
and the bidding is growing, per capita flowing, Man is
going, going
gone! sold to the ghost in the white suit and gold spectacles
for distribution by his middlemen, mind-brokers, the dealers
in reality, his real estate men of the human soul,
insurance agents against the possible truth with words of neon
the tick-tocking, click-slick rainbow sellers with slitted
eyes against the sunlight, peering into briefcases
the quicksilver pickpockets of life whose hands I caught
in my innermost bowels selling my sanity piece at a time
to great financiers with oil-slicks on their brains
and plucked-featherless goose-pimpled once-beautiful
black birds crashing inside their smooth white skulls

III

domes haunt me:
domes of the bald-headed sterile planners of destruction
dome of the skrawed bald-head eagle, destined for extinction
dome of the great white head of Capital, lobotomised, still
ticking helplessly with mono-craziacal monumental
schemes of final devastation
the rockets prepare for rape, the final gang-bang; intercontinental
canniballistic missiles are up,

bursting the seams of the economy's crotch
the masturbation of the dragon, the nuclear smegma
smearing the earth like pellagra
in the Sahara, Pacific, the furtive emissions that leave it weak,
nocturnal semen of an overcharged economy
gotta shoot your load, gotta get your rocks off, baby
per capita capita capita capita capita capita capita!
the missiles blast off in your head
who's dead?

IV

it is a system
is the deheaded army on its way to the job, vampirialised
the day before, at the bloodless battle of 8 to 4
the click-clock clerks whose lives drained into red-ink pens,
scrawling vouchers and L.P.O.'s to keep per capita flowing
it is a system
of lunatics in well-pressed gabardine administrating
ministries, industrial plants and human feeling
the higher guardians of the tomb, the doom-full pyramid
they name society, serving the silent despot of an embalmed past
eunuchs of a dead and secret king
the carefully kept corpse of the American dream,
whose bandages we smell in our children's hair
and everywhere it is a system
is cyclop stares of hydra-headed vision screening you for
entrance to the crypt
is laminated faces, words in cellophane, assembly line of
attitudes, emotions, lives
is: what we do not need.

V

it cannot
dream the juice of flowers into our lifeblood
cool the sky into our drinking cups, it cannot
sustain the human exchange, will not supply

the human demand; it will never draw
sea-rock-sand-fruit-land-woman-man
into a futuriginal circle

VI

it is un-, de-, -less, mis-, non-, nultra-
it
disintegrates on contact with the final question

VII

YOU
are the final question.

Crazy Eddie is the priest
Of a god so great
He rules in every heart
And every state
      (Crazy Eddie)

The god's name is Hav
And he talks to you
Through the voice of Crazy Eddie
Tells you what to do
      (Crazy Eddie)

Crazy Eddie's got inside you
Looking through your eyes
You see everything through sell-o-feign
And it's all lies
      (Crazy Eddie)

Crazy Eddie's gonna get you
Gonna take your soul
Do some fancy mathematics
And then sell it to the world
      (Crazy Eddie)

Crazy Eddie's gonna trick you
Gonna steal your mind
Sell it back to you, reduced
To $1.99
      (Crazy Eddie)

Crazy Eddie's gonna steal
Your daughters and your sons
He will turn their hearts to metal
They'll want the cars and guns
    (Crazy Eddie)

Crazy Eddie's gonna get you
Gonna steal your dreams
Bounce them all around the world
Via satellite beams
    (Crazy Eddie)

Stop! We don't need to do
Another Crazy Eddie rhyme
All that hip-hop rapping
He's just stealing our time
    (Crazy Eddie)

The real point, however
Is what do you do
To overcome the Crazy
Who's inside of you
    (Crazy Eddie)

He's inside of you
    (Crazy Eddie)

He's inside of you
    (Crazy Eddie)

He's inside of you

Well I'm thinking of expanding
Changing my scene
And I'm looking right now
At the Caribbean
    (Oh yeah)

The weather is fine
And business is fair
In fact, there ain't much
Competition down there
    (Oh yeah)

The rum and the music
Are hot hot, hot
Goddam, it's just the politicians
who're not
    (Oh yeah)

You wanna make a deal
Just pay your payola
And everything is easy as
Coca Cola
    (Oh yeah)

Well I'm ready now
Gonna make my move
And you Caribbean people
Better get in the groove
    (Oh yeah)

Gonna move right in
And everything is fine
Yeah I know it's yours
But I could make it mine
    (Oh yeah)

Say, don't you wanna be
An American state?
A lot of others want to
Don't be late
    (Oh yeah)

Or do you really believe
You got some other fate?

BEDTIME STORY, W.I.

watching television
cornflakes cars and clothes
the children finally chose

heaven was on the other side
behind the white screen
so all made a decision

they left this hell
and walked right through
into a commercial about beans

they swallowed that too
then, for the first time, looked
at this new world they'd entered:

coiled quiet monsters watched them
strange cubes like blocks of empty buildings
were crackling a million voices

the twentieth century had outfoxed them
they lost the way home, tried another
then an MGM lion roared and charged

they panicked — some ran into wires
their green eyes burned out from the sparks
some disappeared into transformers

the children scattered, bawling for Batman
looking for Sesame Street
seeking the little house on the prairie

but they were behind god's eye
and it was snowing on the screen
plus, a commercial break was on

a shower of cornflakes fell
some struggled, but you can't beat Kellogs
then it was all over

only one boy returned
into the living room:
now, alone, he stares at his own vision

ABATTOIR

for human consumption, livestock,
red flesh slashed, hang on hooks

above blood, above rubber boots
which do not feel, above the dumb-shocked

throat-cut carcasses that had baulked
all the way, but still went

the cows, goats, sheep, all decently
drained of their lives

and functionally, dying for a purpose
although, alive, they'd never known it

look hard, feel no remorse:
we crawled out from the ice-age

predators, remember? — this domesticated carnage
is necessary, keeps us going

only, observe sometimes your feet walk
stiffly; sinews in your neck

contract; tendons of your life cringe
as you approach the work-place

inside, observe those heads bowed over desks,
those shoulders hunched, those lowing eyes

so bitterly familiar, observe all those
good functionaries accomplishing their tasks

watch the overhead clock, its blades which slice
deep into the living flesh of hours

but who is the butcher? and what is
the purpose of this systemanic sacrifice?

BLIMPIE'S BREAKFAST
(for Charlie Laughton)

Manhattan, Monday morning.
The beast has been awake all night.
It is famished, it can hardly wait.

The Monday people — vanishing into orifices on every street.
A thousand doors, a thousand turnstiles,
a hundred thousand maws open, then clamp shut.

i'm hungry too, i stop in at a Blimpie's:
two eggs on a roll, coffee —
a meal to start off Dow Jones on this working day;

musing, i read my coffee cup lid:
Lift 'N' Tear
— exactly, what else?

Lift 'N' Tear
old buildings, presidents, small farmers ...
coffee's not bad, though, considering all that.

From outside, the crunch, and then the drooling ooze
of traffic, the crackling of people as the day warms up:
Monday, everyone is on a roll.

i finish Blimpie's Breakfast,
a plastic parody of a workingman's meal,
and wonder about Blimpie

— a gourmet, probably
corporate executive, spreading, never quite full —
then i leave.

Outside, i stop to listen:
dreams, someone is eating dreams.

YOUR MAIN STREET ENDS IN SOWETO

1.   you have put your soul
   into the night-deposit box
   tomorrow
   they will lodge it and withdraw it
   they will sign it, seal it, stamp it
   they will send it to South Africa
   roll it into bullets
   and give them to your sister

2.   the steps you walked
   out of your car
   into the bank
   will walk across the sea
   up to the door of your brother's house
   and kick it down

3.   the figures in your book
   think of them
   as statistics of the dead, the wounded
   and tell me again
   how many thousands?

4.   the coins, the silver pieces
   when they leave your fingers
   will close the bulging eyes
   of black, dead children
   who saw too much, too far, too soon
   too late

5.   if you would know
   your signature
   is your soul,
   your work creates the world

the meaning and the shape of it
your self
exists in the simplest actions
the body and blood of each minute,
what could a man
exchange his soul for?

6. silver?

7. you have put your soul
into their night-deposit box
tomorrow
they will lodge it and withdraw it
they will sign it, seal it, steal it, stamp it
they will roll it into silver bullets
for your sister
the day after tomorrow
the silver will close your eyes....

MAMMON

ghost, guardian-spirit of banks, trans-national corporations,
daylight deals in air-conditioned sewers
ghoul, eating the flesh of our dead childhood
ghost, effluvium of the rotting innocence in the skull-vault
ghost, smoke-screen between my self and your self
whose language is a hissing yes to vice
who salivates hypocrisies and sleeks the tongue with moss
who slithers between Man and Woman
who multiplies us only to divide
who adds and then subtracts to zero
ghost, slick as night-wet city streets
vinyl-skinned and glittering with devices
whose rock-pit is a gold-mine near Johannesburg
mammon
watching our children growing
never-closing nickel eyes minting their images
watch him, this god
rattle like dice, like thirty pieces of silver
watch him
flick and rustle a green promising tongue
watch him
grin like a wallet opening
watch him
as he whispers to you now.

BIRTHRIGHT

the people's leaders and the plush financiers
soft in an air-conditioned upper chamber
sat round a mess of pottage

price of pottage had been rising
to match the high demand
set by the Joneses of New York who'd made it;
now the mess of frozen pottage that they'd left
was thawing on the table:
plastic aluminium chrome and vinyl dreams
baubles bangles beads (the very latest)
the head of John the Baptist
other crunchy pieces of the good life U.$.A.
(John Wayne eats this too and so does Marilyn)
happiness with added preservatives
were all there for the taking

the leaders, sitting on old promises, shifted
uncomfortably; their pulses quickened
to a disco-beat; they watched
as bits of pottage gloated to the surface
they calculated ballots, checked the G.N.P.
(a former loud progressive thought about
the ancient bargains on the Guinea coast)
they phoned a subcommittee, consulted an expert
grafted a proposal, then
negotiated on the terms of trade

question marks, percentages, mark-up figures
clattered like thrown dice on the table
rates of interest flickered
digits registered in pale eyes

papers rustled stiffly with secrets
attaché cases lay like open traps
lips unzipped halfway
tongues retracted their positions
and as they fixed the price of pottage
the air was crisp, metallic
tense with the cachinnation of betrayal

finally they paid for pottage
with the sun, passing it off as a gold coin
they paid with stolen diamonds of clear singing rain
with brand-new banknotes of the young leaves
they used the pearls of our women's smiles
the silk of rivers in sunlight
pure silver of fish in the free ocean
they hurriedly exchanged the stars
for genuine low-cost sequins at Carnival
and hustled off the new moon as a tropical curio
to Mrs Jones' boutique, N.Y.
they haggled, bargaining like vendors
till they were bartered down
back to their last, their final good —
their people

the flushed financiers added one more clause:
blood for Coca-Cola
one brain for each Gestetner
Jello in exchange for semen
a talking blue-eyed doll for each one of our women
Bargain! Deal! and then, the best part —
a pocket computer in exchange for a heart

silence washed in eddies through the room
bald heads bobbed in it wisely
a corporation chairman asked the time
one politician stirred the cold mess thoughtfully

an expert dipped, sampled another morsel
said it was delicate, in his opinion, but
(eventually) worth it
so
the people's leaders, in the upper chamber
broke bread, broke faith, poured blood
and minced their words and our flesh into the pottage
then they began to eat, slowly, without appetite
their last supper.

A VILLAGE GUIDE (IF YOU RETURN)

i

Return to D'Ennery, you will find
a village like a chronic sorefoot,
the same one street like a used, unwound bandage,
homes clotting the raw flesh of hillsides.
Development schemes have cauterised the hillslopes
and they are waiting for the zinc ointment,
the sterilised white dressings of some
industry or other, some light manufacturing, some
fly-by-night concern, a factory, a hotel, can't-tell-yet —
such things go by appointment
and it seems D'Ennery was late
or else too patient, like you said.
The dust from bulldozers, years ago,
clearing a bypass to the industrialised south,
clogged the pores of plants and other things
and after the machines grumbled away
there was a stunned shocked silence.
Even the blank sky could not believe
there could be more of nothing.

ii

At midday, white anaesthetic light
cuts cleanly between buildings, spilling no shadow;
a dog's bark snaps the day in two
like a bone breaking.
                    The broken day
clatters open like a smashed calabash, exposing
running eyesores that infect the tourist industry:
two drunkards, sagging over a draughts board,
nowhere to go, they've used up all their moves;
sprawled on the church-step, Labadie, laid-off since last year,
yawns at the wide stretch of the day;
a child crossing a bridge stops, stares at

27

the river leaking like a wound turned septic.
Midday: each slit-eyed home looks like a private sorrow,
a grief that formed a scab but never healed.
In D'Ennery life has the colour of old houses.
Inside, behind the jalousies, on the thin partitions,
pictures of the Sacred Heart, the Last Supper;
portraits: Agafa djamet on her first communion day,
Son-son who never wrote from England,
Jerome, living in a jail in Castries.
Portraits, dust edged in a frame of passe-partout.
Midday: sun like a torturer's white light on them

iii

Return to visit D'Ennery if you must:
those who are born there leave.
It is too bare; rain or no rain
there is a drought, an absence
of a feeling of protection.
The furry tongue and sour breath of a long illness
has licked at everything; the bush,
wiry and defensive, straggles up the hillside;
the goats there scramble for a foothold
trying to take root; even the children,
footloose already among rocks, laugh at that stubbornness,
even the children...

iv

Return. Perhaps you'll see
something i missed, perhaps the rain
may have a different meaning when it falls
or you may smell some other thing above
the gangrene of political neglect,
the white priestly reek of funeral candles.
You may even think that what the sea
is moaning, what you hear is not
the litany of the defeated, the waves of groaning

28

penitence repeated in the church at vespers.
Perhaps if you return you'll find that crippled village
only in memory; perhaps things may have changed,
i don't know: what i know
is the helpless understanding any poet feels,
that words are only miracles after all,
they heal by faith — and who believes
a poet?
        Perhaps you'd better stay.
If you return you'll only find
what you have learned and taught me
once again — that for a place like D'Ennery
words are like sea gulls in the rain.

* djamet: St. Lucian Kweyol word for 'whore'

CASTRIES

(for John Robert Lee)

I

i came upon this town

i came upon this town while she was changing
out of her cotton country Sunday-best
into synthetic pearls and leatherette;
stripping off delicate, eaved French architecture
to struggle into high-heeled blocks and functional pillboxes.

Everything was changing:

people, the way they walked, why,
how they waved at you
more and more from a passing car
going who the hell knows where — it ceased to matter
after a time. The very language changed.
Even the river festered to a swamp.
The stone lions on the bridge started to lose their teeth.
Then someone closed the wharf from where i used to watch the sunset
making miracles with water, a few clouds and a sea-gull.

It all happened so fast:

i was talking Creole love-talk to a girl just down from Morne La Paix —
we finished, bargaining how much it would cost, in American accents.
i've probably resigned myself to it all now
except sometimes — like on a day when rain
blurs everything else but memory — i remember
and, in a French ruin overtaken by the coralita
or a girl i knew from Grand Riviere —
Solinah, whose voice still makes a ripple of my name —
i glimpse her again, naked and laughing.

Labyrinth

Streets misleading back into each other.
And walk or run, i end
where i began. Lost
in the city's changing ways: the labyrinth.
No matter how i turn, it's the wrong way.

Always, i meet the desperate others, the sleek skeletons
that tick to work, tack home
clique-claque to church and back
who balk, always, at my simple, single question.
Always, this econometric ordered panicking of people
distracted in the whizz and ritz of their own static
frantic and wandering the maze of licit trafficking
blind to the cloud of furious black flies
that buzz and drip over a something
stinking already somewhere beyond the next high-rise block.

Always, all day this white noise
hazes the undersound:
the gnashing of the predator, the victims' groans.
Somewhere within this, the minotaur
paces, trampling our scattered bones.

III.

Queen's Lane

1.

The last of daylight flickering between
old buildings on the oldest corners
downtown Castries: Queen's Lane —
quiet now, so different from
when sailors came there raucous and swaying off their vessels
in that time, in my childhood
when my father was a sailor
in the girlhood of the city, in that time
when Castries was a virgin too young for the twentieth century
and even whores were innocent, seen in our light.
In Queen's Lane now
which was a pale, dim imitation of a red-light district
the sunlight splutters like a family lamp
and goes out, taking those times with it.

Those times, that age
illuminated in the memory now as the wick of the horizon smoulders,
as clouds absorb the light like lint
and birds fly home, crossing a hillside
and the city — drained empty of its flow
of trafficking all-day shoppers, workers, hustlers, the usual
busy flotsam bobbing in the drift of commerce down her streets —
stops, struck by the sudden, momentary inwardness of things
and feels her emptiness.
In that pause, her straight streets curve
into the few forgotten side-lanes left
questioning themselves where they are going
and as this happens, for a while
it all seems possible:
the hills around her hold the fragile city in their arms
and she is Blake's Jerusalem.

2.

Night, and all this goes in up a
blast of sodium vapour lamps along Bridge Street.
Along the blocks, store windows open fire,
staccato volley fusillading the main street;
the evening is rapidly strafed by street lights;
the first few passers-by of early night,
caught, are raked in the crossfire.
Inside the show-windows corpses are already stiffening
into grotesque statuary like bodies at Pompeii.
They wear ghastly smiles;
they don't know they are dead.
The ones who come out afterwards take them for mannequins
until, staring a little closer,
they meet ghosts coming at them through the glass,
then they too fall into the windows soundlessly.
On the main street a long block of buildings, Khronos & Sons,
its long line of show-windows railway carriages,
shudders, jerks into life, moves off slowly,
bearing its bizarre cargo without motion toward nothing.

3.

Later, as he does every night, the watchman,
following his shadow, crosses the empty main street,
listening, watching, trying to understand
a journey without footsteps, the mark of feet....

        In Queen's Lane now, dark
with history, not night,
he switches on his flashlight,
hoping for revelation, something to explain
his city crossing from one age to another
within moments, without meaning.
The light does not work.
The past, a lost frightened child,
draws even deeper now into the dark
here in Queen's Lane.

IV.

Koo

The city's streets construct a maze.
i walk them all ways, all hours, but i can't get out.
Yet i know these corners, the veins in the sidewalks,
these old houses that have outlived fires, hurricanes,
hurry-get-rich property developers, the rage for progress.
And from a child i've known this
stubborn, greying house on Brazil Street
and in its always open doorway
this stubborn, greying cobbler: Koo,
patient as the precise, measured taps of his hammer.
Koo, eking the waxed twine to the hole
he pierces with his awl, drawing the line through
just like when i was small and he had told me:
"There's a right way to everyt'ing."
As i walk past, in mid-life no longer sure about that,
he taps another nail into the sole.
i watch him, hunched still over his last,
pulling the taut twine home, tightening it — a final knot.
Then he replaces hammer, knife, wax, line, awl
back on the shelf.
He is an ikon. Seeing him, I see
there is a cord i need to find,
a kind of line — strong, supple, like what cobblers use.
i need it: to walk the city's inner maze
to find the minotaur and yet not lose
myself.

Ti Jean

This country-bookie town turned city
too fast for itself; at night, it's nervous.
The reclaimed land it's built upon
winces from the touch of water underneath
the streets, the stores, the parked cars — empty.
Watchman, these steps you hear are yours,
walking the ways the others have abandoned.
A silence follows you, gulps your footsteps,
swallows the pale, shallow puddles of your flashlight.

Listening, you walk, searching
for a greener town, a barefoot child you half-remember.
But among the city's blocks your shoes talk
to themselves. Whoever paved this place
paved a whole life under, made it hard.
No foot can print here.
No hint of your early, unshod self
can mark that slick, implacable surface
you walk, mute, flashlighting streets, stores, parked cars — empty.

You'll find nothing here.
To find that self, you must
leave the main street, go
round that bend you recognise from childhood, turn
left, leave Jones & Co., Barclays Bank, the temples of Hav,
round this last corner, down this last backstreet to
the dead-end of I. Moffat Ltd.
        Here
in a gutter gorged with the city's hawk-and-spit
the full moon
flickering in the muck like a dropped coin.

A memory, quicksilver, startles the mind,
("Kenny, you lose your mother's money!")
reaches your hand, before you realise it, down —
to meet your dwarfed, distorted image in the gutter, changing
into a child, rising toward the surface,
the moon clutched in his hand.

Watchman, switch off your light.
This is the child you left
barefoot among bulldozers, barbergreen machines, the beasts
       of progress;
the child outside the maze, abandoned
as you, and all the others, followed the blueprint lines
into the labyrinth your town, your heart, became.

Look deep, this is no twitch or flicker of a fantasy.
This is a child of the Imagination, Ti Jean,
breaking the clagged surface of memory,
sounding from stagnant water of your too-long silence.
Look up. He's given you back the moon
that you may walk again. Truly.

HOME ECONOMICS
(for Wendell Berry)

1. *Value*

In those days all shops were called Ma This or Mister That.
One shop my mother used to send me to was called Ma Branch.
i'd go, playing with my shadow all the way,
trying to outrun it on the Methodist church wall,
dodging it away from other feet — or suddenly stopping it,
chanting my list meanwhile so i would not forget:
1/2 lb. saltfish, 1/4 bottle oil, 4p. keg butter, 1 blue soap, 2 cough drops
over and over till i reached the shop.

Of the two ladies selling, i liked the tall, dark, gleaming one
whose face i later recognised in Benin sculpture.
She would set the things down one by one
gold, blue, lemon, dark-white speckled shapes, smells, rustlings of paper
until i had a heap of pirate's treasure on the wooden counter.
Then she would slip the pencil from her hair,
tear off a piece of shop paper, make a rope ladder of figures
and i would watch the pencil climb, drop, climb, drop.

Ma Branch didn't sell; she sat down, buxom and comfortable as a barrel
amidst a larger treasure heap of bags and boxes, packages, cans,
not missing a thing, collecting money, talking with customers.
Some women came with notebooks and no money — regulars:
"Ma Branch, on Friday when the man get pay...."
and sometimes a child, whose mother couldn't write,
would speak up, too loudly: "Ma Branch, my mother say..."

Ma Branch had a miraculous set of balances in her head
in which she weighed each separate request
unhurriedly. No one ever took her for granted. Yet
i never saw her do otherwise eventually
than bob her head, to one side, to a shop lady
then nod, once, the other side, to an expectant customer.
By some commonly held scale of values, now so strange,

37

she gave all of them credit.
Fascinated, i'd hand over my money, wait for change
then race back past the church wall, followed by my shadow.

Years afterward, when seeking the darker shadow brought me home,
i heard that she had died.
There is a supermarket on that spot now — it's larger, well-arranged.
But it can't fill the space she occupied.

2. *Price*

At the supermarket, i pick — from a shelf, of course —
a fruit i haven't eaten, even seen, for a long time: apricot.
Soil, sun, rain, wind, the work of hands
and an impenetrable mystery
have shaped and sweetened it
into a small, brown, sentient globe, a round of life and death
complex and whole as our earth its shape reminds me of now.

The store attendant weighs it,
placing it on a scale connected to a calculating mechanism,
taps the right square keys
and extracts from a whispering slit in the machine
a strip of pale, adhesive paper, printed with digits.
She sticks this like a plaster on the apricot.
So now i know, she knows, the cashier knows,
the owner of the supermarket knows,
in fact, every potential buyer (except a child or lunatic) knows
the exact, precisely calculated price of this strange fruit.

At my turn in the queue to the cash register
i pay, then i receive —
it is the stock exchange, the standard intercourse of our times.
what i would like to know, though,
what i would like to ask the shop attendant is:
In all of this, what is the unseen, festering wound
that she has tried to cover with a plaster?

BRIDGE

From this side of the bridge, at night
the town's a video game. The street lamps shoot
at crisscross crazy cars that dodge, hoot,
blur, flash out of sight.

There is a toy-mad conjuror somewhere
practising sleight-of-hand with people.
In your own eyes, they dwindle,
then they disappear.

The car ahead that pulls out with your friend
winks a sly red eye at you,
then speeds up, taking him for a ride into
a dark with no end.

From the old side of the bridge, you wave.
He won't come back. To you or to himself.
The bridge within is gone. Tonight you feel a gulf:
It's yourself you must save.

STONE

(for Maurice Bishop)

1.

No elegies, no elegies.
They'll only help us to forget,
only ease the pus from our consciences,
only bandage our suppurating questions
under a soft, sterile silence.
No elegies, please, no elegies.
It is better our sores stink,
that they fester like Lazarus,
better our maladies are noisome, that they clamour,
that they swell and bloat and burst
or they will never heal.
He was a healer, Maurice was a healer
and he needs no elegies.

2.

What now — a public statement on Grenada?
We leave that to the manipulators, the manoeuverers,
the managers of public righteousness
who, the next day and the dark days following,
spread their smear campaigns on lavatory newspapers,
distributing the droppings of a two-ply president,
Goliath, champion Philistine, boasting from Gath,
broadcasting mankind into camps,
spitting out stars and stripes by short-wave radio,
swearing blood-red pure-white and true-blue justice
against a David daring to dream a bridge across our enmities

3.

No statements — they are too final to be true.
When he died, questions
flew out of his broken, bulleted body

and hovered overhead like blackbirds.
If his body held an answer, a public statement,
it was never found.
So now what Grenada says to us
is private, we can only hear it
one man, one woman, at a time.

4.
It is not political.
It begins
where slogans can't be heard,
with simplicities that are too deep
for projects, conferences, development plans;
it will not be reduced
down to a dialectic, no ideological brain-scan
will reveal it, it is not political.

5.
He must have known.
He was a healer, like Toussaint, he must have known.
Dissecting with a surgeon's eye his people
into capitalist, lumpen, petit bourgeoisie,
he must have known
that amputations would be quicker
but that he would be left
for life, a nation aching with its ghosts and absences,
grieving its gone lovers, friends, relations, even enemies:
a maimed country, a war veteran, feeling still the lost, lopped limb.
He must have known
the gap he tried to bridge
was wider than what gulfed Dives from Lazarus.
The schism between Right and Left, between even his comrades
and himself
was older than the rifts and harsh volcanic fissures of his island.
He must have come upon,
deeper than history, wider than theories can span,

that chasm in the mind of each of us,
the edge, dark,
where we leap, falling, into Man.

6.
No elegies.
i'm glad his body was not found.
We would have buried all his questions with it.
His death was like a stone
and we may carry it, heavy in guilt
for our apartheid while he was alive,
for our sneers and our sick silence
while our leaders lie-belled him into a leper
or we may clasp that death inside a sling of questions
and, with a faith in the impossible and in ourselves,
fling it, true, to the giant's head
as he had.

7.
His death was like a stone
into the great lake of our soul; it stirred
strong, spreading rings of loss and anger from a common centre.
Years later, this evening
a nation's memory shudders, rippling the Grand Etang;
in Fedon, a lone cinnamon tree
shivering; a felt absence quivering its branches.
Wheeling above it, restless, rising
against the picture-postcard sky over Grenada,
piercing our silence,
a shattering, sudden shock of blackbirds
scream, keening their dark questioning words.

I

island in the sun
my father's hand
stained with your soil
has never owned you
so, i am claiming you now
acre by acre
dream after dream

(*As morning breaks the heaven on high*
I lift my heavy load....)
that sun, that fucking sun:
our sweat would turn to smoke
dreams bake down to stone —
that was the heavy load we lifted

and we lift it still

island in the sun
'discovered' by Columbus
devoured by the British
'recovered' by the French
stripped and searched by Spanish not-so-noblemen
uncovered for the touch of merchant Dutchmen
passed across tables
hidden in the silken sleeves of statesmen
island
stone that the builders refused

but we lift it still

(*I see women on bended knee*
Cutting cane for their family
I see men....)

living and dying, it was cane
only we could know
how bitter it was
how deep its roots went
those women knelt
to feed a dragon —
there was no family
only successive crops of children
reaped
crushed
distilled
till the ratoons exhausted themselves
into dried old women

II

and year follows year
wet flows down to dry
cane fields lie fallow
some die, some flourish again, some spring up, lives later
as ghettos, estates where nothing thrives
only acres of zinc, little plots
of misery and endless waiting
here and there, a patch of hope

o island island
the shackles and shacks
the treadmill of history turning
the dragon's teeth still gnashing in the factory
the white trash of the lives left
to the survivors
the shreds, the people of straw
like:
the alcoholic, who sets his glass between us
and curses
the whore, the abscess between her thighs;

curses
the sisters, their vices wrapped in hallelujahs;
curses
the madman carrying hell in a bag;
curses
"de whole rotten dutty stinking dutty John Crow life."

bagasse
                    debris
                                        detritus

III

children of Sisyphus
children of Cain
children of Rum and Coca-Cola
always asking:
who will roll the stone away?
Listen.

I say this stone is
a foundation, is
a new bedrock for the newborn
this stone
can slay Goliath
it is his headstone, flowers will grow from it
it is the dragon's final stumbling-block
his millstone, it will crush him
this island, this stone
hides a shape the world has heard of
never seen:
a man's shape, but more truly
prepare: we will soon break the stone
            we will soon reveal him.

DE LAND — A CARIBBEAN NURSERY RHYME

Is de land, de land, de land.

Cause anyhow you check it,
eat food raw or open a can,
is from de land you get it.
You paper and pencil, pot and pan,
calabash, coalpot, everyt'ing we got,
is from de land we make it,
is from de land we take it.

Is de land, de land, de land.

We cyah live in de sea —
dat for fish, not for we.
We cyah live in de air —
we eh put nothing there.
We doh have wing or scale,
we eh monkey or whale.
Zoo Story - Ja '76 109
We is woman and man —
we must live on de land.

So if dat is de case
how come in dis place
you find people who roam
who eh have no home
with nothing to give
and nowhere to live
who sleep under truck, under tree
yet is people like you and like me?

Go ask dem why, you go hear dem cry:
is no land, no land, no land.

But I doh understand.
Look it there all around.
It all on de ground.
But I notice big people does say:
dis big piece for dat big man dey
and dat piece for dat other man.
But really I doh understand.

And dey have a lotta signs that said:
'Trespassers will be prosecuted'
by some feller who call himself "Order"
who have land from border to border.
All that is bad enough, I find
but at least he could have another sign:
'All the hungry must be fed!'
cause if you stay hungry, next t'ing you dead
and nobody want to lay down and die
rich man or poor man, you or I.
And I want you to tell me
(and doh tell me no lie)
if Order can have land
then why can't I?

It eh he-land, or she-land or me-land.
Is we-land, is we-land, is we-land.

Cause anywhere you stand,
is we great-great-great-great gran'
black woman and man
strong, proud African
who plant it and reap it
but they couldn't keep it.
Now their bones in de ground
dat we walking on.
All their sweat and their toil
gone down deep in de soil.

We cyah leave dat for Order.
Dat's like selling we mother.
So we have to demand
dat he share out we-land.
Otherwise it go be
all for him, none for we.
    Pa ni doubout an péi-a
    Pa ni doubout an péi-a
    Pa ni doubout an péi-a

And da is trouble. you see!

*Kweyol: In our land it have nowhere to stand.
(a chant from a children's game played in St. Lucia.)

FASCIONERS OF PROGRESS

Because you do not heed the voices of Imagination,
neither the tongues of trees nor the voices of poets,
earth will erupt in a conspiracy of poetry and nature.
Earthquake and landslide will snap and grind to rubble
your Baal-high idols of concrete and metal.
Fire will shrivel the prefabricated palaces
swelling like boils on our inflamed land.
Wind will shatter the thin cocktail glass illusions of our progress
into glittering dust scattering
over the ruins of casinos and the high-rise cemeteries made low.
Sea gnashing at our degraded shoreline
will foam corrosive spume that will dissolve your headstones —
they will return to sand.
But the poet's words will last.
You will hear them prophesying in the hurricane,
their warnings in the night-sea whispering towards your chambers.
It will be the poet's words coming at you
in the thundering sermon of the landslide,
in the revenging wind swearing down through the valley,
the crackling of the sun gone wild.
And when the earth has had her say and retribution,
afterward, in the green time of healing,
there will be other words, given to other poets.
They will be precious stones with healing properties;
mixed with dirt, folded in leaves and used as poultices,
they will protect the children who recite them.
But these words now — are for you,
David-stones, found at the river of reflection
and gathered in a poem, ready.
Come, fascioners of progress, come.
You hold the steel cuffs of the law,
 the silver coins of bribery, the gun.
But when you see a poet writing poems,
run.

AFTER THE ELECTION

Finished now.
No more loud speakers, snarling knots of citizens
yanked right, rushed left, but finally drawn backward.
No jeers, no squabbling horns, no party hacks
to split the blue night with political curses.

It's done now.
Not a politician. One time there were dozens,
each with a different line to lead us forward,
all trumpeting their sides, leading their packs
nowhere. All that, for better or worse, is

over now.
Tomorrow, jobs for jabals, barkers, third cousins;
dump the used ballots, whitewash the walls, it's not God
who wrote there, just people. Yet, in the world of acts
that writing matters, unlike these verses

that end now.

POEM IN A MANGER

where is the poem?
not on this page i'm looking at and reading from.
where is the poem?
not here, not in these miserable words i'm writing now
though i have to write them, though you have to
read them, see them, hear them.

cause really, if i could, I'd make this page
howl at you, the paper burn crisp, the letters burst
like pustules and pressurised blood vessels, so you would see
on opening this inadequate irrelevant book
flipping this ridiculous bit of paper
not a poem
but a baby blackening and charred and smoking still
cindered by its private holocaust-to-come.

if this baby
(that's its ear you're holding at the corner of the page — let go!)
would curl and stretch and stiffen
one last time like a burnt page in a still wind
if this baby
would show its blackening sooty teeth
like letters hitting a page
without a   w   o   r   d
if it would turn over on its back
contracting to a bitter foetus, regretting every screaming
moment it was in the blank book of the living
if you'd see this
hear this, touch the wincing flesh of it
just as you turned this page
if you'd see — goddam it, why don't you! —
that the baby on this page, disguised as a raving poem

is you, really all the time is you
then how
would there ever be again another war
another flash of nitroglycerine
another tin soldier flashing tin-medalled teeth
another jackbooted 'yes-i'm-ready' puppet in the box
another and another and another and another
walleyed uniformed somebody's son to press or pull or push or ram
the triggers, switches, levers, plungers, pins, paraphernalia of the
weltering world-waste of another war?

how would there be
if this baby, swaddled in words, lying on this inadequate page
would burn alive
before your eyes and howling all the time
that it was you?

if you would see, then you'd see why
the poem isn't on this fucking page
then you'd see where the poem has gone
and why i'm trying to use these useless goddam
words to catch it, and
why i need you to
help me do that

look at the page again:
these are just words

let us go find the poem

ALL THIS IS LANGUAGE

(for Ayodele and Idara)

This, all this, is language:
a sullen mob of rain distant and murmuring
wind whispering low rumour in the bushes
clear shout of light over the hill.
The earth is utterance:
hosanna! is the scattering of pigeons
hallelujah! stands the tree in the noon hour
selah, the psalmody of waves in the late afternoon.
Branches like epileptic prophets in the wind
gibber wild questions at blue silence
and the taciturn ground, in sudden joyful places
cries: chrysanthemum! rose! bougainvillaea!
i listen, half-remembering....

The river, talking often in its sleep
a long sentence, an incantation
of silver and white feeling tumbling too quick for thought...
damn, the river makes no sense at times
but words are like that
especially when spoken, like wind and water words.
So lately i trust the rocks especially;
they write their messages.
They intend, like all the ancient poets,
their words should take the weathering
of time, stay true as epitaphs.
Awed by that vocabulary — of things themselves —
i am illiterate, dumb before them.

This morning now, raw wind tearing away leaves,
the sky unscrolls
that puzzling calligraphy of clouds again.
i shake my head, turn to

the rugged cuneiform of dry-river stones
quick script of wind on grass
blackbirds printed on blue morning
all, everything, like ciphers in a code
hieroglyphic messages i used to know....

On days like this
i try to read the earth-poem
but a scrawl of haze, a smoke
from something charred, but smouldering
sneers over the landscape.
Singed, the young grass twinges
memory, the scent of childhood insidiously accurate
rises acridly and stings.
On days like this my eyes run
and everything is blurred.

OASIS

So much more true, the understanding without words.
After all, the words trekking this page,
following each other like pack animals,
groaning in syllables under their burdenings of meaning,
will lead you, if you follow their uneven caravanserai, finally
back to an understanding which is oasised in silence.

In that void waste, the oasis, open-eyed,
dreams an original memory of garden
before the beasts and you heave into sight
with trinketings and bellows of demeaning speech.
For one clear moment, that single eye
will hold all, even you, even the animals,
silent, in an encircling vision.
Then you will thrash in, fevered, jangling, thirsty
and drown the moment of your revelation.

Afterward, shouts, questions, orders, curses,
words creaking to formation, a struggling line,
pack animals looking for an oasis again.
But why do we always leave the true, Edenic silence?
Why did i write this poem?

PRINTS

These are not words. They are the tracks
of yet another traveller losing his way
in the white waste of Lectin's land.

Look back. Already, you can trace
how each firm line of footprints
meandered back; then, tentative, the fresh marks...

This traveller wanted to go east
beyond the strict edge of the mind,
to leave the level, dry, dead sand

of the bare intellect. But: the bright glare!
So brilliant he went blind. His journey scrawled
inexorably south. Look, word after word

shows how he drifted, till he fell — here.
White sand absorbed him, leaving only a blurred dent.
His prints read clear, though. He was lost.

As we are, following his trail,
tracing these tracks which cannot lead us home.
It's not that words fail. It's that we are not meant

to stay in Lectin's desert, on the page.
Even to reach the east, to cross beyond, over the edge
is not enough. We have to rise

into dimensions where the words disintegrate
to their original being,
a place where, beyond language
beyond thought or sign or emblem,

we look downbackward watching our footprints
meandering a white desert of unmeaning
struggling in tentative dark hints
towards a poem.

Between myself and poetry, there's a barrier —
the desire to make poems. Intent on this,
i do not see the gloss that words make
on reality; how they silently slice vision
into things, into what the eye can take
for granted. Making the poems, i miss
poetry, the sudden light that breaks
even its own limits and transforms
words into worlds and worlds into itself without distortion.
Instead, from all those brittle poems without poetry
i have built the subtlest prison, an Eichmann's glass box
of words. Inside, things come to me
refracted. i, in turn, become a curiosity
vaguely deformed, a thing even my wife calls
a poet.
It is one of the few words that can send shocks
jarring through my celled self; i hear it
loudly; it makes me see
that i am not; there is a pane
i see things through.
A real poet, when his voice is true
shatters that glass, his words disintegrate
his poems disappear, leaving the clarity of poetry.
i've never done that.
Something that does not trust the naked eye,
that turns words into theorems,
lives in here with me. One day, soon or late,
i'll kill it. But now, reflected in these glass walls
of words, i see it
writing another of those 'poems'.

THE MUSE'S COMPLAINT

Albertina say:
i want some other rhythm
dis one cyah make me
break away
an' i tired dancing waltz.
Look dey!
You see dem children?
if i only coulda
rock like dey rock
(and den)
dip back and jerk
(like dem)
you know i woulda
free up me mind,
is such a long time
i want feel like meself
again

some other rhythm
some other rhythm

i doan want to tell lies
just the truth as it is
woulda alright wid me
but i cyah hear it right

(some other rhythm
some other rhythm)

Albertina, Albertina say:
i want some other rhythm
because dis one too light

dem make it too tight
it noh free
it eh me
it too slow
it cyah show
all the things that i be
so
i want some other rhythm
dat will free up me senses
break down de fences
(just take a look at dem
children dancing)
some other rhythm
dat goin' rock to de bottom
of me.

LAST WALTZ

I   waltzing Mathilda, waltzing Mathilda,
square dancing, measured 3/4 prancing
and may God save the Queen....
       can the new rhythm ever
       break out of these bars?

       so far, waiting
       not creating
       anything,
       so far, the void before the voice
       the waiting for the waltz
       to end

       but it goes on
       circling la-la la-la
       bringing mi right back to doh,
       and here's Mathilda
       dressed in white
       smiling tightly
       tripping politely to me
       once again

No! No! No! No!
even my feet say no,
see them stamping?
they will break her
if she makes another
false step, waltz step
towards me, they will trample her
my steps are earthquakes
my anger is another rhythm,
now....

II   dancing another dance
from i couldn't tell you where
not here
but i dancing, and
is that i want so long
so long i waiting
for the different rhythm
for the walls to crumble down

III   and is one good t'ing
'bout dis ya music:
walls come tumbling down,
you rockin out de
message of you body
burnin' slow a fire
down below
until
you really catch!
you dance like a burning bush
your feet prophesy
the new ways, and you go
your movements flowing like
you always did know how
you woulda reach
to where you always know
you had to go back to...

tramplin' Mathilda
tramplin' Mathilda.

LA BELLE DAME

love, i must confess
for years I've known
a fiery mistress
all-consuming woman

she told me choose
between your life
and hers; lose
love — or my life's truth

at first i laughed
then went dumb
my tongue chafed
no words came

she says my voice
requires your death
love, i refuse
i need you both

love, in my faithlessness
bear with me
no woman's merciless
as poetry.

TRADITION

once, as a child
i opened books, hoping
each was a casket precious with words
thoughts that had sapphired in the dark
deep underground in a man's mind.
i searched for feelings that had crystalled
into language — a word like 'lust'
winked like a ruby in a navel,
'mystery' was an emerald, laughter' was amethyst
and once, i found, and then i lost
a strange word, one without facets, whole
almost beyond utterance and uttered best in secret:
the word 'peace', like a pearl.
when i was young, i never wrote a poem.
words flickered, beautiful and wild
in their closed cases, bright with the richness
of their makers' minds
and, as a child, it was enough.
i played, and then returned them.

i don't recall
when i became a thief
or why (perhaps losing that pearl?)
i made my head a casket, locked up
the wealth of meanings that i had not mined:
words are the only diamonds you can't steal.
Now the words rattle in my skull
loaded dice in a cracked cup
and i'm afraid to throw them
and there is no way to return them
except sometimes, as now,
within a poem.

ANTONETTE'S BOOGIE

i could do wid one o' dem boogie tonight
a deepdown spiritual chanting rising upfull-I
a Bunny Wailer flailing Apollyon with a single song
i could be in a mystic dance tonight
when every tramp i tramp I stamp de dragon head down into hell
and every high step lifting my leg one more rung upon de Jacob ladder
and dark as de place be, it have a light
it have a light, sweet Jah, more beautiful than fire!

i miss dat kinda boogie tonight
where your heartbeat is de bass-line
and everything so still within de centre of de music
although to an outsider it sound noisy
but doh mind, out dere is de wilderness
and here alone in dis place is de voice of prophecy
wailing in de reggae riddim for our time
telling us to flee, to forward, doh look back
and wo! right in de middle of de song
Bob singing stop — de rams' horns start to wail
and dis dance-hall is an ark
dis dance become a journey

One o' dem kinda dance i want
where flesh to flesh is serious business
where de rubber and de dubber making one
a dance where music is priest
and de deejay from de tribe of Levi
and all our voices from de valley of de dance floor
rise up in jubilation everywhere upspringing children of Jah
chanting psalm unto psalm unto psalm unto psalm
night into morning, praising and raising every heart higher

until de light
and den we sight Jah face

i miss dat kinda boogie tonight
where de dance-hall is a holy place.

ANGELS
(for Frank Banton)

Even in New York, angels.

Most of the time they fool me.
i think that what I see
are birds and children twittering all over Central Park,
not cherubim.
Or, those are just clouds
caught with an eyelash flick
in trees, blazing in sunset,
not seraphim, flaring hair flown back, riding the wind —
not in New York.

Although
my woman and i once, night-walking
down between the hulk and mass of the harsh canyons of commerce,
rounded a corner   and met the moon
laughing as she rose, clear
out of a narrow crevasse in between two banks.
Still though, it feels stupid
talking of angels in New York.

Yet if it isn't angels,
why is it
that in the rumbling belly of this white whale,
in its tortured twisted intestines of subways
there is, sometimes
one moment
when the giant worm-tracks are silent for merciful once
without the sound of one blind burrowing scavenging worm
either coming or leaving,
when even the yellow stink of piss goes quiet

and, warm above the heads of the suddenly mute travellers
waiting for something that could really take them home,
a full gold angel's song is poured out
by an ordinary, slightly scraggly modern Gabriel
holding an angel's horn of plenty —
or, if you like, a dented pawnshop tenor saxophone?

REGGAE CAT
(for Boston Jack)

Something
in the way these alleys twist and
drop into darkness, how they zag
around a corner, jump a ditch,
rub against a zinc fence as they pass
quiet, quiet, avoiding the street-lamps,
telling you ignore the brightness,
trust your feet, you won' fall, listen
to the brotherman ahead of you,
he knows the way, he eh go let you lost —
both of you going the same way, don't it?

Something
in these alley-shapes, the dark, the scratch
of footstep   pause   a matchflare
catching the bass bearded voice within
the circle in the yard, within
the sweet smell of smoke saying
peace and love, mi I-dren, peace and love

Something of all this
stretches your sinews till they become guitar strings
trengling under the chop-and-slash
of fingers ratcheting at chords that cry, like
when love hurts you, like
when a lean, lost alley-cat, twisting in her heat
starts wailing:
          skeng-ek
          skeng-ek

A CARIBBEAN ROUND

Josephine Jacobie
born on a Monday
seduced on a Tuesday
feller left Wednesday
they put her out Thursday
she get a job Friday
the money done Saturday
she cry all Sunday
the baby born Monday —
What you think she call the baby?
Josephine Jacobie

LITTLE JACK HORNER

Finger in every pie
chairman of committees
fund-raiser, advisor, organiser, patroniser
good boy, always got the plum.

After management studies
junior partner, Piper & Co.
pies monopolised him
fruits of success hypnotised.
He painted himself busily into a corner
looked through myopic eyes
at a vague wife, a daughter, and Jack Jr. —
they seemed unorganised
in fact, unmanageable.
Baffled, he plunged back
into a buzz of phone calls, meetings, files.
Up to his arms in deals
he pulled another plum.
But with such eyes
how could he see
that it was dark with flies?

OUR DAILY BREAD
(from a Manhattan sliced loaf label)

Give us this day, America,
enriched flour, reduced iron, niacin,
mononitrate, riboflavin, thiamine,
vital wheat gluten, monocalcium iodate,
vegetable shortening, corn starch, calcium carbonate,
potassium bromate, sodium stearoyl lactylate,
partially hydrogenated soybean oil with mono-diglycerides, dry malt,
water, yeast, sugar, salt.

Amen.

Sell by
July 4.

DEDICATION

may this poem
be a path of bougainvillaea
brilliant on a dark hard hill

may words of it
petal this common ground we walk, lost

may flowers of its faltering syllables
bleed to some clearing

its scent — of something true to its own being —
lift through our thicketed dark speech
and undergrowth of silence

may this poem
leave us traces — sparsely —
along this strenuous heartland
as (stubbornly barefoot, barehearted) we walk

toward an unforeseeable place
a flickering grotto any moment now
that shrines the meaning, then suddenly so simple,
of our difficult love.

VILLAGES

you see, i've always wanted us to be coincidental
that love would
like village corners, contain and meld
our separates, yet
not fuse them

i crawled, still crawl
patient towards our true footing
urging, yearning it
to be the reconciling curve
of morning village paths
meeting
not the harsh intersections
and naked angular conflicts
of tactical city streets

but then, you're different,
salvaging our peace
from driven, head-on crashes
i want
no crossroads' clashing dictates:
unity or crucifixion

i think
until we come
to those quiet-streeted villages
and, cornered by love, learn
the natural curve that turns
our flight into direction
till this,
all other meeting
separates

MADRIGAL

you know
dem times dere
when you try to say things
   with your fingers
   the palms of your hands
   your bodyweight
all your soul tryin'
to squirm into your groin?
'cause words
have tricked you before
cyah trus' dem no more

in dat time dere
your whole body
  becomes
a coherent poem,
but she can't see the theme,
  just likes the rhythms

    so you end
     on an
       apocalyptic
        downbeat

    nothing said

    you know
    dem times dere.......?

ISLANDS

from halfway in my mind
somewhere between where
i want to be
and what i have become
i write you

i can't ask you
to come down please and see me
i don't know how i even reached
here, islanded on my own life

the tides from all around are coming
in, only in, they never leave
from this rock, never flow to rescue —
nothing, no way out

the white teeth of the waves
all day chew patiently, all night
diminishing the headland gradually.
i have gone in further

now here, halfway between
the innermost high mountain
and the soft temptation of the sea,
looking away, rigid, facing neither
wishing these words were strong seabirds
wishing we weren't islands
i write you, because
that is the one way out.

MONAL

O the howl of it, love
the keening after you
long tunnel of dark without a glint, without
a any slit of light of you,
the days like knives.
and i am listening for your smile in the air around
longing a letter.
                only rain
the insistent hush of showers
admonishing against the house
messaging on roofs, at windows cautioning
'keep your pain
quiet, quiet....'
raindrops like proverbs in the mind,
last night the new moon taunting again.

O love, the left of it, the achening
the hungering after you-not-here of it
the not, the perhaps-never of our arms legs woodbined
together, the too-continuing journeys that assail us
love,
the gone, the bone-close absence of you
is with me here, ghosting my efforts to keep live
veiling faces, strangering each thing; even
the acrid, smoky reality of words
is filtered; they taste and smell
of absence, love
the missed of you, the far, the lorn in every quality,
how everything
is distant! the hand not ever really
holding things, not really

this leaves me
wilded over, wound and
twined like intestines around this O, this nothing-here
leaves me
oval spaces to fill
whole skies that i must spread with markings
or blot out into
and i begin to doubt

these longer days awaying into distance
leave me wondering
even tonight i glimpse
the lean dark body of my longing
impaled and bleeding on the horns of the moon.

HARP

we've made a strange instrument
a harp with a single sound
high-strung across the archipelago.
a catgut heart-string feeling
strains across a thousand miles.
at night, the sea
thrums with our single twang
crackling moonlight; the bright splinters chime
(the jade and ivory fragments wince
into the memory, sink to our sea-bed self).
twangling a blue note
sea ripples with our plucked moan.

     still i try,
remembering our songs,
to strum for harmony —
there's none
no other tone can come.
this steady, lone vibration
meets yours in a groan
songing over water; we tell,
in terrible unison, of separation.

     now someone's struck
the white gong of the moon
and set the breakers shattering
they hiss like tambourines.........

sea shivers under our messages, tonight.

the cold blue truth of our music
stuns me.

　　　　monotoned by absence
the toll of each day
i wonder (but it's useless) how
to unstring finally our harp tonight,
let the strained tendon of love
rest.
but i play on, a mad musician every night,
a psalm of un-hope, tendering you
to helpful waves, good tides
(no crosswinds i wish you)
and a harbour of love
elsewhere if so.

in the morning
moon falls like a stone.

ALMOND

you could have given me, if it was all you had
the crushed core of your need
it would have been, that kernel loneliness,
for me, a dark beneficence
more beautiful, more welcome
than the rain on dry days

why didn't you
give me even one tamarind seed
of your sharp, hidden hurt?
instead of our cracked shells, dried fibres of old fear
we could have had that,
something to exchange the taste of, to feel
that this at least we both know

yet i can answer better what i ask you:
you, all the time, were wanting me
to break the almond of my silence
give you even the sour sea-grapes
of a life rooted in sand and shaking in sea-wind,
sardonic fruit, but you'd have eaten it
(you told me after)

it still seems strange i never knew
and i am still ashamed
that acid grapes, the acrid flesh of almonds
were what i had — even now
are what i have

but why we never shared our bitter fruit
is a mystery to me now.
what else have men and women ever shared

since that first moment in the garden
when — forget what happened after
it is not important
what is important is
it was the first time —
a Man and Woman trembling in taboo
tried with all they had, with what they knew
to share, death though it was
the thing that mattered deepest to them

too late now
i give you
the broken bitter almond of this poem.

each time i see blackbirds i remember you
that road, that day:
'de female is a sort of brown, not really black —
ah look!"
a blackbird plummeting in front of us,
skimming away off to our right.
'a male' you said.
it was evening and the birds were going home
skyfire flared our shadows close, ahead of us.
we, in the darkening coming on
walked a strict path of affection
a byway, like that one, fenced off on both sides
from the wide fields swelling into hill and further up to mountain.
jet-black questions flickered in the mind, veered off
swooped in again :
how much to take, to tell you?
how much to give?

walking, following our shadows, going
to where the by-path met the main road,
we still talked about blackbirds
(something frantic beating in my chest).
watching birdflight across field, into trees
i wondered: why don't we jump this fence?
go where the bird goes?
why do we always take the main road?
to go home?
questions winged us, scattered from the night now coming on.
soundless, the two shadows flew ahead down to the road.
we pecked among our words, cautious for answers
as the hovering night spread down and settled
(some desperate thing still fluttering my rib-cage)

i meant to ask: are blackbirds faithful?
always go home to their nests?
why is the male so dark?
but the answers mattered.
i felt the questions clawing in my throat
until we reached the main road, then a van came
just as a sagging line of blackbirds broke, crumpled onto a tree
and something beat my rib-cage
and went quiet.
then we got in

we still have not reached home.

sweet chile
dem will say dat
dis eh revolution, stop it
dem go talk about
de People an' de Struggle
an' how in dis dry season
t'ings too dread, too serious
for love

as though
love not a serious t'ing
serious like war, frightenin'
tightenin' de heart strings an'
beatin' a rhythm up a twistin' road
all o' we fraid to dance on

love is a serious t'ing
bringin' you back
to baby-helpless trusting nakedness
whether you want or not
if in truth, in real truth
you love

a serious, serious t'ing :
is walking a high high edge
where looking down or back
would end you
yet forward and up
so dark wid no end
love is — o god sweetheart, dey mus' know!
dey can see!
dis instrument we tryin' to make — society

economics — wood and string
den politics — de major key
but de real, real t'ing
de reason an' de melody
de song we want to sing
is love
is love

come doudou, sing wid me...

GOOD MORNING, THERE ARE NO OBJECTS

i woke this morning
the taste of silence
smell of banana in the room
the memory of your breast like sapodilla in my teeth

no objects in this room
no thing more real than the other
the table waited, breathing
the chair sat
quietly, saying nothing

the bowl too
was saying nothing in particular
it only said banana, orange
and its perfect mouth
dilated slightly when it said
pineapple

sun-shaft, breaking darkness
at the one crack in the louvres
shattered silently into photons
and scattered the sun-seed
deep into the corners

the house ached with the night before
you could have walked through
walls that were walls only
out of habit
yearning for the single, the separate
soft sex of objects with the light between them

last night
has left the whole house dipped in milk
i feel the nipple of each object
if i rub the light switch one more time....

you burst like grapes in my memory

and everything is rounded
i find their centres without thinking
now, as yesterday and all
the other flattened surfaces
curve backwards into spheres and crescents
i swing upwards again like a bell's tongue
laughing inside you.

WATER-WOMAN-POEM

Whether this is a poem about love
or poetry or landscape, i do not know.
i know that from the disparate elements of our lives
we somehow make a poem;
that from my silence, isolate as mountain,
and the torrential rains of feeling falling in your words,
we make, without any intending, a landscape
more than mountain, more than rain.
love, without you i would be adamant shape,
rock-masculine, renitent, graven
to idolise the limiting necessity of form.
Yet without this barrier, perhaps
your nature might be spent against itself,
water falling on water, fretting in waves, rising in restlessness again.
Instead, out of our meeting, rain and mountain, we are changed.
Rainfall by rainfall, riven and baulked,
we yield into a rivulet,
then, as my resisting substance gradually gives way,
our issuing river, enscaping earth and water, unreeling out
like a long unpunctuated line of some ecstatic free verse poem let loose to go
wherever its joy takes it (form and content and content and form inseparable)
flows, while growing things — wild plants, wheeling planets, love songs —
follow our sinuous dance down to the sea.
But, like i said, whether this is a poem
about love, landscape, poetry....

VISIONS OF US

as an old couple
soft in each other's presence,
a living humming with the quality
of those village stores you hardly see now.
Bags of sugar with clusters of bees on them,
a smell that is the smell of everything:
onions and flour, saltfish, rice from Guyana,
the light — if i could just describe the light
and how protecting it was when i was a child,
how magical an onion bulb could look
on the grained gleaming counter.
Shops like these buzzed with conversation, hefting of boxes,
the thwack of hatchets into codfish bristling with salt,
stories continuing from the day before, the deep dizzying
smell of women full of man and child, their skin shiny with life,
dark in a golden light just beyond touching.
The shops held all that — comfortably,
like a sack casually holding 100 lb. of potatoes.
There's no word for the subtle grandeur of such places.
Always, you miss it, like you miss
the ordinary massive beauty of the diurnal world.
But that quality, vast richnesses in ordinary things,
is what I see
in visions of us, years from now,
as an old couple.

THREE SONNETS FOR MISTER KENT

DELIRIUM TREMENS

Towards the end he got the d.t.'s. He would see
a smiling girl in a white first communion dress
waving at him. He'd smile back, point her out to me
and i stopped arguing because she, more than i, could bless
even a little, those last days when my presence
only made heavier a weight of guilt and love
that he was tired of. He turned to her, his innocence,
he turned to her — with joy, the way he would have
turned to me, his son, if i had known enough
to see, past a son's need, what he was giving:
his rebel walk, trampling all boundaries, and his child's laugh
bursting like fireworks, igniting from a flame of living.
i grew too fast. i never met, in me, the child
he later raised from his own need, who waved and smiled.

'SO JAH SEY'

Dread song. 'Not one of my seed' the words said
(and it hurt every time i heard Bob sing)
'shall sit on your sidewalk and beg your bread.'
No, Pa, i'd think, never. My eyes would sting.
And yet it could have happened. Easily.
i burned to live a different kind of life,
more wild, more free — in fact, the kind that he
had lived, even with children and a wife.
My simmering rage would boil sometimes, would spurt
hot scalding words on him. i'd almost leave.
But i knew he'd turn beggar. And that hurt.
Why? Pride? The thought that when he died i'd grieve?
No. But somehow he had become my son,
my seed. And i, a tree now, couldn't run.

MISTER KENT

My father left me the city's derelicts.
At thirty-one, it was a strange legacy:
whores on their last flare, bums, alcoholics,
the smell of rum-and-cigarette, poverty.
An acrid smell that i could recognise.
But there was something else as well.
They had a burning. It inflamed their eyes.
Their look could scorch your world to hell.

And yet they called me Mister Kent.
And the muted warm way they said
it breathed a bright blaze from that patronym,
illumining for me what his life meant
and why, although in one sense he is dead,
in a new light i have inherited him.

BROTHER BONE

Not just brothers, we were close.
Death, first son of my mother
and I, we made one.
As eldest brothers will, he'd constantly advise,
prod, goad me toward my good.
He was brusque, even mocking, but without guile.
Most people found him hard; in fact,
my close friends called him Bone
(secretly) and told me he was too exact,
severe in his perspective, he was cruel.

Perhaps he was, i never noticed.
i followed, hero-worshipped him because
he was calm, wise, deep in the ways
of everything which lived — each leaf, bird, beast
or man. He taught me how to see.
There was a clarity, each thing was haloed
when Death, my brother Bone
pointed it out to me.

i never was alone.
i loved him, for his cold light that showed
the truth in things.
i miss him now.

GULF

He is a crowd.
He carries an internal clamouring
of slogans and labels, the pro- and anti- noises
of the hottest and the latest causes.
But in the centre
is a space of silence, a dark O
from which fault-lines radiate, cracking fissures through the mass.
In sleep, that dark extends, the silence
seeps through his capillaries, his million words congeal
to one sound, one, just beyond the strained limit of his listening.
That sound is all. For want of it,
slogans proliferate, spawning their opposites;
true causes, generating and degenerating words, twist into lies.
For want of it, he wakes and stares into
the deep, cold silence of a gulf
which he must fill with loudly clashing words
or fall, vertiginous, into himself.

ABSTRACT #1

Afterward they couldn't stop talking:
'But he was so nice, I woulda never think
that it could happen to him.
No, not to him.'

And a lady said:
'I wonder why. He used to be so quiet
normally...'

But that was it. The quiet.
Or silence really. When everything
that had a sound, the scream of traffic
the blasting from religious campaigns and political crusades
later, the conversations of his friends
eventually, even the truest music
said nothing.
            Either he was deaf
or there really was, somehow, in all this noise
a silence. Whichever one it was
when he spoke he couldn't hear his voice
and so he screamed — for one whole day
till they put him away.

And just the following week they said:
'But what was wrong! What got
into his head? You sure he didn't smoke
that thing?'
            No, he just saw red
in every thing. The petals of hibiscus
bloodstained the dark earth. A blade of wind
would leave the flamboyant in shock
at its own dripping clotting on the dirt.

Each person, everything seemed wounded: love hurt
and lovers suffered from internal haemorrhaging
helpless to staunch the flowing
of each other's needs.
Each day he watched the sunset.
'It bleeds,' he thought, 'the whole earth bleeds.'
Yet no one saw all this apparently.
Things were just black and white
to them: 'It's you, your mind that's red.'

Perhaps he believed them
or he hoped to trace the artery
to the mind; or he saw the whole thing
as a gift, a necessary offertory.
Perhaps he thought he was
an artist, standing before the unforgiving
silence of a harsh black and white abstract
and slashing on a laugh of loud bright red.

dis dungle dread say:
"Lion!"
flash de colours
carry thunder on him head;
any heart-dead weak-eye
who try shake him faith
or break him righteous roots
him quake dem;
dis dungle dread roar:
"Rastafari !"

red-green-gold rainbow
lif' up from Jamdung
scatter de white thin clouds of heaven —
rest in I-tyopia...
but right now, right ya
earth weird
creation scared, it turnin' colour...
red-green-gold rainbow
dis man a-look a swif' way into Zion.

spliff use to take him dere
before —
but wha'?
spliff turn a white bone in him hand
rainbow faith bleach down,
city dry him roots to straw.
him still sight, but no lightning;
and since all man a-tell lie
tell him own eye
confuse him,
dis man start wear dark glasses
and checking out de zoo

lion dem roar like thunder;
dis dread
him head well knot-up
consider dat dem both from dungle,
him wonder;
'dis a de zoo?
den a which part I-man free?
dis cage ya mean captivity —
fi who?"

him sight!
lightning in a lion eye
flash green-gold-red
and dis dread
again now find him rainbow
so
him climb dis last bright hill
down into Zion
him answer:
"Rastafari!"
to the charging lion.

JAH-SON/ANOTHER WAY
(for Jah Howie)

I

who was born, not of a virgin but a real woman
whose father vanished like the holy ghost
who walked the usual crooked mile
out from the high wild mountains of green childhood
down through the mono-crop plantations of the schools
and out into the alleys short-cuts back-streets
sidestepping from the blocks of bank and church
bypassing glass doors glaring windows, watching his reflection
blur into men and manikins arranged inside
dodging the traffic of emotional commerce, the
blaring smiles honking handshakes of the
up-and-coming-at-you 1600 cc. boys.
who ran from three-striped foxes
taxidermised lovebirds and sunday citizens
who was jobless, had no fixed abode
who slept in fishing-boats and therefore under stars
whose mind was a tenement-yard of heresies
his head a shaggy thundercloud of darkening questions
his beard glistening with treasons and with ecstasies
who had burned churches blasted government buildings
and grown a garden on their waste —
all in his head
who one day abandoning the highway scramble for the golden fleece
went on to seek the lamb
whose name was Jason till he came to know himself
and then became Jah-Son.

II

but where you going, Jason?
look you mudda crying
your brudda an' sista trying
to get some sense into your head

but dem cyah penetrate; your dread
too thick and knot-up; too much o' tangle
mangle-up question clot-up like bloodstain drying
in you brain — Jason, you go go insane!
Jason, you go dead!

III

> **there has to be**
> **another way**

>> 'Too dam' lazy! Ain't he is a carpenter?
>> So why he doh fin' work?'

> **there has to be**

Oh god Jason, not now!
You cyah just leave me now!"

> **another way**

>> 'Come brother, will you give your heart
>> before it is too late?'

> **has to be**

'Comrade, the struggle needs
a thinking man like you.'

> **another way**.

IV

Jah sey
Jah Rastafari sey :
see I trod
through valley
see I trod

102

through town, through stinking alley
see I search
for you
for youth who search
for truth
see I trod
come
I make Man
into God

an' dem a-step outa de shitty
dem vank
lef de school, lef de church, lef de bank
lef de people mek o' concrete and steel
who divide and subtract but cyah feel
de yout' ban that
dem noh wan' that
dem mash it on de ground
as dem step outa de town
outa Sodom and Gomorrah fi go higher!
dem a-shake de city dust offa dem feet
an' a-flash dem natty dread inna de street
dem a-chant an' a-wail an' a-hail bongonyah
Jah-Jah children trod creation on a trail o' bloodfire!

who wan' go
will go
who wan' stay will stay
whatsoever whosoever will

there is a hill called Zion
a sinking ground called Babylon
a so Jah sey

V

a so?
a really, really so?
a two years now Jah-Mighty
an' i still doh know.

here: no cement, no steel
yet something cold
no clock, no wheel
but something
turning wrong and going back.
chaliss burning in my hand, but still
something that i doh hold
something in i know
this not the way

but where to go?

VI

out of the forest, leaving
the twisted track that snaked through bush and coiled round hill
and never led to Zion
turning his back
on blighted gardens, broken earthen-pots
on songs that quavered and then gradually had shrilled to quarrels
on praises that became as thin as smoke
he went down from the psalmist's hill
without hope, not a toke of ganja
nothing to draw on
but himself

VII

down into Mammon's kingdom: among the derelict the broken the insane
the ones for whom the city's alleyways are made, the back-road
side-street shit-lane people the shanty-minded and the minds like cul-de-sacs,
the shingles of dismantled person the 2 x 4 existences of shaking age with

newsprint peeling off their cracked skins letting in the cold draught of
the cosmos, among the dead-ends of socio-economico-political processes
the snuffed-out butts of a city's nervous smouldering, Jason among them

has to be

VIII

his life resembled theirs now, driftwood.
crosscurrents, ill winds of circumstance
would drag him to a sand-spit of existence
another fool of time who'd lost his substance
and the way home.
he looked on at the dredged and dregged survivors
heard the future like the rumour of a storm
and the present a loud silence.

this?
another cripple at the pool?
and yet how to shout "No!"
to the enormous opening mouth of Nothing?
no way?

no way

IX

he lifted up his eyes, last time —
Zion hill was green and far away.
his gaze dropped to his feet:
barren sidewalk, thin-lipped gutter, asphalt street
and saw grass
and saw how earth itself had shifted, split the sidewalk
how seeds exploding in green flame had caught small fires
all along the cracks and weaknesses of urban surfaces
grass laughing fiercely everywhere once you were looking for it
Zion, shining where it had always been, will always be
NOW, no other time, no other place, NOW

NOW as the grassflesh blazes into singing
splitting the sealed-slab silence of blind city sidewalks
and rustling, passing the word downwind along the pavements
illumining, witnessing your metamorphosis

Jah-son.

BEARINGS

I

at certain times, at certain distances, all islands are the same.
coming out of a drift, not sure of anything
any land is welcome :
shelter, a rest from calculating constantly
the pull of cross-tides, the directions of the wind.
after the never-stillness the always-moving waste
you want, more than anything else,
to rest, to stand one place where everything is named:
this is an almond tree, this hill is Morne Lapé.
what do old people say? — sea has no branches.
can you name a single wave you ever saw?
at sea for so long, most of my life
any island was a home.

adrift and off-course, strong dark wind blew me to St. Mar—

how long i stayed there.... memory wavers
like a long swell, pauses, comes at me again :
a terraced land, ordered, hierarchical contours,
reclaimed at its periphery from the sea.
streets. buildings. wires. parks.
signs and directions everywhere

PLACE DE
LA BOURGEOISIE

THE COMMIE
SQUARE

PROLETARIAT— 5Km

HALT
NO LEFT TURN

THE STATE

the clear precise glare of the afternoon
each sign standing stiffly near its shadow:
after the sea, St. Mar– was full of certainties.

guided by signs, i walked one-way streets
entered buildings, arrived at my predestinations
only i met no one, no person, not a soul
i saw THE PEOPLE frequently. but always far off.
in all that time, i looked for someone
to tell me, or to listen, if not answer
this: who had made these signs?
had they ever been shaken by wind? or strong rain?
what if they fell?

but i saw only signs to speak to.
THE STATE kept throwing my echoes back at me.
i grew quiet, fearful of my own voice
          until the night
my head rattling echoes like a box of seashells
i shook it, desperate, shook it! — till they fell
silent; then each shell, each questioning echo
sounded with waves, with many voices, with the dialectical
eternal questioning and answering of the sea.
the sound of water, restless, talking to itself in waves
was constant after that — it entered everything.
reading the signs aloud, all i could hear
were breakers, far but clear.
sometimes i could swear, (sunset, before the lights came on)
the island was afloat, and drifting.
          i could not stay
and after i had lost my way, in daylight, twice
one night, i took myself and cast off from St. Mar–
watching its ordered rows of lights dwindling behind
sailing into a coming darkness.

II

McNeil, it's no joke i tell you, being lost.
it is the first touch, first fingertip
of something intimating you with your mortality.
words on the page are much too ordered to express it.
besides, words keep together, they move in lines
in definite directions. even a single word
is a clustering of syllables, letters at least —
the exceptions always are disquieting.
one of these now — the "I" — relentless in its singularity
becomes a hieroglyph of contradiction.

I
am a drifting mote on the horizon line
mast of a small craft lost in immensities of water
yet, because the sea hates its own formlessness
that sole speck becomes the centre
of what is otherwise a vast waste.

at sea you are twice-lost. the ocean searches
even more than you do. time elides
into water, you lose it in the flow
and, knowing now how fluid is the fixed world
how islands of meaning disperse into cloud
you finally accept: this craft must be your home.
meanwhile, you must sustain your self, so
starved of meaning, i
begin to fish.

the strange fish, the deep ones
prefer the night, without even the moon
with just the deliquescent light the sea distils
when something stirs the surface ...

a long wait
then i throw the line, a filament frail as faith.

my steel hook, a glinting question mark, disappears
hoping, inside the silent moving dark
taut with my hunger, my wish that one night
following a line of poetry i will catch
a strange quicksilver being flashing in the depths ...

McNeil, you may be right. perhaps the poem
is the necessary light to search by
(f)or the Light itself — on this you're not clear.
can a poem be
an article of faith, a prayer?
can poetry, out of sheer despair
become a psalm?

III

in the dark
the hole the hook made closes over.
the ripples disappear, like generations,
into each other   as disappears the mind
calmly into its own full emptiness
around a centre seen only by imagination

in the dark
the voyager scanning for signs, thoughts that wing over the head,
a black-and-white bird glimpses across
hangs for half a moment in the wide sky
drops, and wheels over the waste:
                  I!
half-cry, half song
above the drift
                  epiphany
                        it vanishes
in the dark, a poem
like a mermaid singing
comes to guide me.

WANDERER

night
wide-world-over darkness
not one star
only the lighthouse and its lonely flame

from house-windows, this
is picturesque, or even comic.
to lovers on the shore
romantic, a subject for a poem.

for the seafarer
seeking the island in the dark
this single eye
is all

guide
glint of home
a god who winks
a strange approval of the wanderer.

LECTIN'S REALM.

be careful here, the skull caverns:
mist, haunting down the river
curdles with a touch the quick flow.

here, strong feelings bleed, blood turns to lymph
a glaucous slime subtles on everything.

the river glowing from the heartland lags, slows
down to a gelid, hydrocephalous lake

in which phantomicites leech and suck
the open dreaming eyes of children

their dancing limbs, their hair, picked clean, plucked
by the intellect's white corpuscles like piranha.

light here glitters: something with blind diamond eyes
refracts the early truths into uncertainties

and further in, the frozen dreams like stalactites
accuse and gore the mind.

a glazed gaunt landscape of ravined things
dried ecstasies, the ripped entrails of innocence

bones, bleached bones of Ovalea's children
white on the river-bank like shards of moon
the only light.

here, an ulcerous landscape feeding on itself,
is Lectin's realm.

following the river, the seeker
must come here; he has no other choice
to reach the lambent sea clear as a child's dream
whose far voice, like an undertow of memory,
has trolled him here.

SAND

Dear G —
i have reached the place you spoke about
so many years ago. Like you, i cannot name it.
No tongue can lift that word's weight.
It is not strange no one has ever
screamed it out, ever whispered
what it is; there will never be
a language that can claim and hold
the horror of this numb.
But this is the place. i know
by the way the mouth has dried,
the heart has shut, the mind is dumb,
just like you said.

And i've begun to wonder: how long
did you stay here, waiting at just this edge,
before retreating? G——, let me admit, while i've the chance,
i once subtly thought less of you for leaving.
Here now, i see it wasn't (as i'd thought) a jungle fear
of what you called the uglies in yourself —
twisted desires, slithering and rutting in the mind's mangrove —
but the shock of desert, the sudden absolute absence

of this place, this blank and nothing of unfeeling sand,
this knowledge, simple and irreducible as stone,
that alone i'll fail this necessary journey,
this dwindling belief of ever meeting
a one who will companion me beyond the edge,
this watching myself lose, gradually,
even a sense of loss.

This is the place. i understand
why you turned back. But how i wish
you'd found, or met someone who'd found
a way across.

CAVE

Haunted. Your head a bat's cave of scattering thoughts,
glimpsed-gone-again; haze; a smell of excrement.
The life unlived has caused this,
has wraithed, mephitis from the bowels of your being,
eroding out this hollow in the head
where your own dead words echo now,
reverberating into sentences of self-indictment.
Too late. You waited.
You waited far too long. You should have seen
that those dark questions, hanging
would one day flail at you, a bristling crowd
harpying their Why, Why
crowding the cave with echoes, with shatteringly loud
shriek after disembodied shriek of I, I, I, I

Strange, that you are the only one
who hears all this, who knows
how the next scream could send you
battering your own head to jolt the bats out, to kill each thought
hurtling at you out of the miasma of the unlived life.
And strange too, that the only way out of this cave:
is to be still;
to overcome the shrill, assailant voices:
is to be silent.

But stranger still is how you know
others have lost themselves in this dark place
and, beyond echoes of self-mockery and despair, have heard
eventually, a silence more eloquent than word
inseparable from the light that came, filling this haunted space
until they saw themselves and found the way to go.

A CARIBBEAN EXORCISM POEM
(G.C.)

zombi
is the thing we didn't do
words unsaid and roaming
the life we never lived

bolom
is the hope tormented, unfulfilled
shrivelled to a premature old man
in a baby's body
stillborn, still unborn

demon
is dissatisfaction in a mocking shape
the leer of years
contorted grin at ourselves, laughter misused
and coming back at us

and i am the devil
gored by undeeds, prickled restless
by a life that roams inside
despite
a mouth to say it, hands
to shape it

devil, beelzebub, devourer
head-haunter howling in white spaces
serpent, unwanted whisperer
is (if i know it)
the other brother of myself, returning
a difficult counsellor
tortured paradox
eternal parable of our need to love.

C

For E.M., in homage

At that time, Lectin
was a seer, a serpent.
In the beginning, poised
like a hand lifted in benediction,
facing the Manowoman.
In those unclosing eyes it seemed
the One reflected in two images.
Manthought: which of these...?
Womanknew: there was no way to speak it.
Lectin, troubled, wishing its eyes could close,
said: i will tell you
how to tell him.
There is no him, she answered.
He has forgotten, smiled the seer,
we'll have to teach him.
Show him this fruit,
break it,
ask him to try to make it whole again
and tell you what it is.
He'll understand then.

But the man looked at the fruit
intently, squinting through half-closed narrowing eyes
and when it broke, the sudden light
splintered his strained seeing: he saw   things.
He took the woman for his shadow, and she said:
No. Look. i break this fruit
in two. Which
is the shadow of the other?
She thought: he'll see.
And, simultaneously, she knew:

that Lectin, intending love, had cloven them.
 Man   / Woman
In time they would cleave again
and whole the world.
But from Now, from Being, Manowoman
shattered in two thoughts.

Desperate, she ate her half, she urged him:
Eat! we still may...
But by then he had begun to name things.
He named her:
Eve
and loving him, although she knew, she answered:
Adam
then they were truly separate.

The serpent, trying to unsay its blessing,
split its tongue
and then, transfixed by contradiction,
the duality of the intention and the act,
trying to vanish time and matter, thought and word
into the beginning again,
started, in sacrifice, to swallow its own self,
beginning at the end.

LIMINAL

evening
the late sky is rinsed of cloud
hills are shuddering lightly in a wind
drawing their ruffled burred coats a little tighter round them.
this time of day, this light
the mountains have stopped climbing
they seem to slope, heavy dark slumps of land
as though earth herself is letting go.
in the fold and groin and contour of her hills
the green is growing into dark
flowers dim, like freckles of a girl becoming woman, leaving
only hints of what they were, tinted on darkness
the veined sky tightens like a stretched skin
sunset dries out in daguerreotype.

since childhood i have done this
watched the day end and the night come
and tried to draw a line between them, isolate
the moment, hold it
with my will, the whole bent of my self
but i have never: now i seldom try.
still, without intending — following a felt urge —
i can't let many days go by
not watching the sun set.
i distrust the theories and book-answers that I've read on this
they may be right, but they may misconstrue me
i only wish mysterious evening light
would, one day, pour its darkening clarity through me.

VILLANELLE FOR BLAKE

for the searcher, sunset always is a sign
by its fading and its brilliant light he sees
life is a ripening unto wisdom though a slow decline

night revellers laugh at sunset while the lonely pine
but neither yet has understood its mysteries
for the searcher sunset always is a sign

the blazing sun in dying makes the cold moon shine
action, reflection make our lives dualities
life is a ripening unto wisdom though a slow decline

thus wise men look not with the eyes but with the mind
between the shadow and the light they find their certainties
for the searcher sunset always is a sign

day into night, good into evil intertwine
they cannot separate and be their own realities
life is a ripening unto wisdom though a slow decline

and so the seer upon his deathbed, knowing all divine
sings to the dying sun bright angels' melodies
for the searcher sunset always is a sign
life is a ripening unto wisdom though a slow decline